ROCK BAND CAMP ALL ACCESS

VOL. 2

TODAY'S HITS

PARTS AND PLAYING TIPS FOR THE ENTIRE BAND
GUITAR, KEYS, BASS, DRUMS, AND SINGER!

ISBN 978-1-4803-5127-1

HAL•LEONARD®
CORPORATION

7777 W. BLUEMOUND RD. P.O. BOX 13819 MILWAUKEE, WI 53213

Visit Hal Leonard Online at
www.halleonard.com

Home

Words and Music by Greg Holden and Drew Pearson

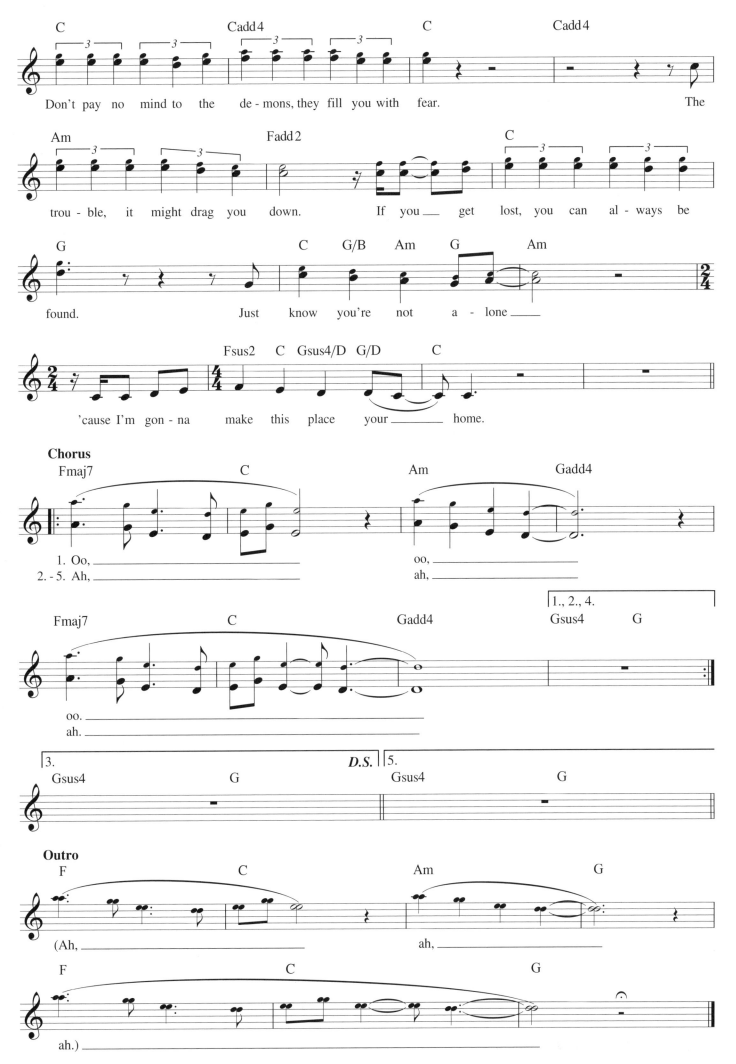

Don't pay no mind to the de - mons, they fill you with fear. The

trou - ble, it might drag you down. If you __ get lost, you can al - ways be

found. Just know you're not a - lone __

'cause I'm gon - na make this place your ___ home.

Chorus

1. Oo, __ oo, __
2. - 5. Ah, __ ah, __

oo. __
ah. __

Outro

(Ah, __ ah, __

ah.) __

3

Guitar

Home

Words and Music by Greg Holden and Drew Pearson

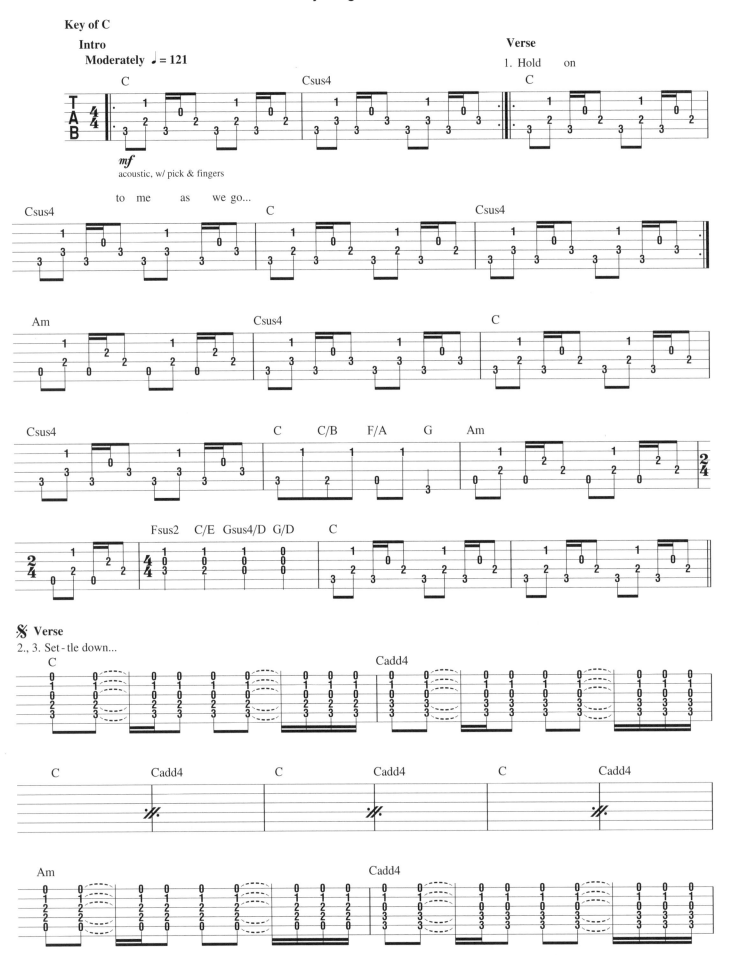

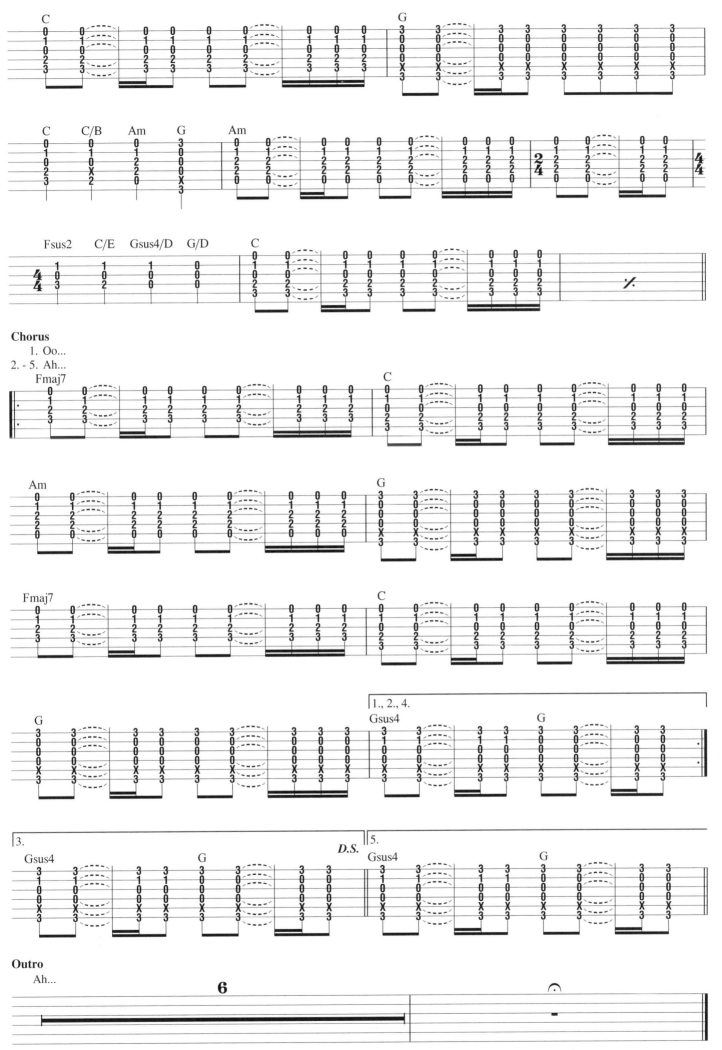

Chorus

1. Oo...
2. - 5. Ah...

Outro

Ah...

Keyboard

Home

Words and Music by Greg Holden and Drew Pearson

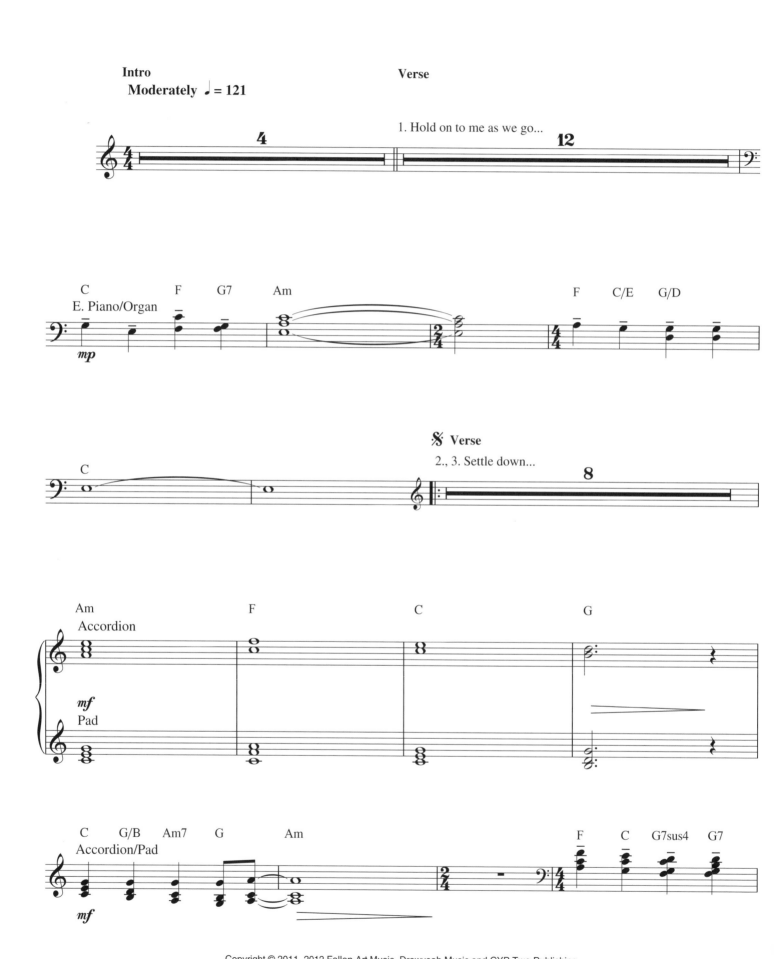

Drums

Home

Words and Music by Greg Holden and Drew Pearson

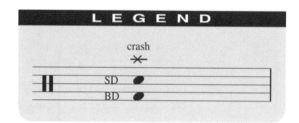

Intro
Moderately ♩ = 121

Verse

1. Hold on to me as we go...

𝄋 Verse

2., 3. Set-tle down...

Play 3 times

Chorus
Oo...
(𝄋) Ah...

Play 7 times

To Coda ⊕

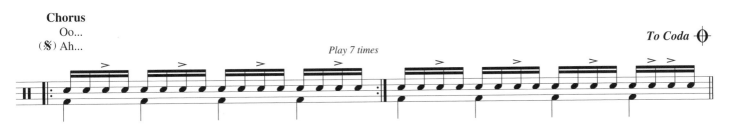

Chorus
Ah...

Play 6 times

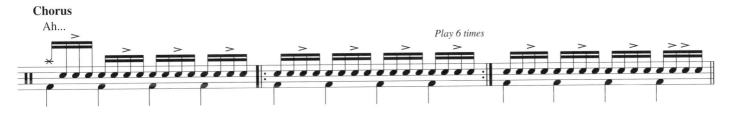

Chorus
Ah...

Play 6 times

D.S. al Coda

⊕ **Coda**

Chorus
Ah...

Play 6 times

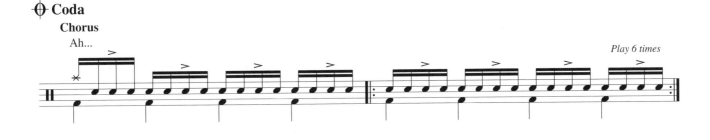

Outro
Oh...

6

Bass

Home

Words and Music by Greg Holden and Drew Pearson

Key of C

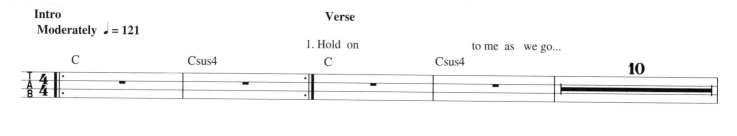

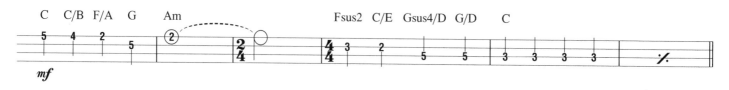

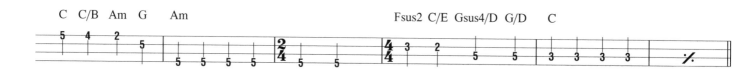

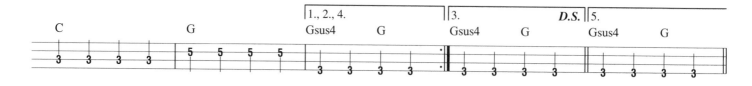

Locked Out of Heaven

Words and Music by Bruno Mars, Ari Levine and Philip Lawrence

Guitar

Locked Out of Heaven

Words and Music by Bruno Mars, Ari Levine and Philip Lawrence

Key of Dm

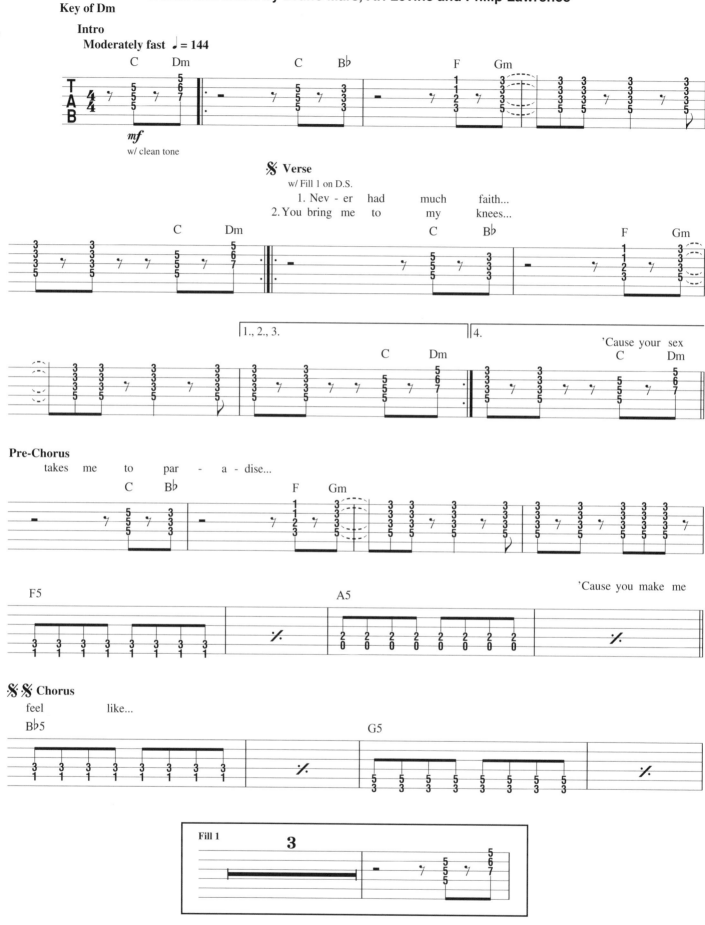

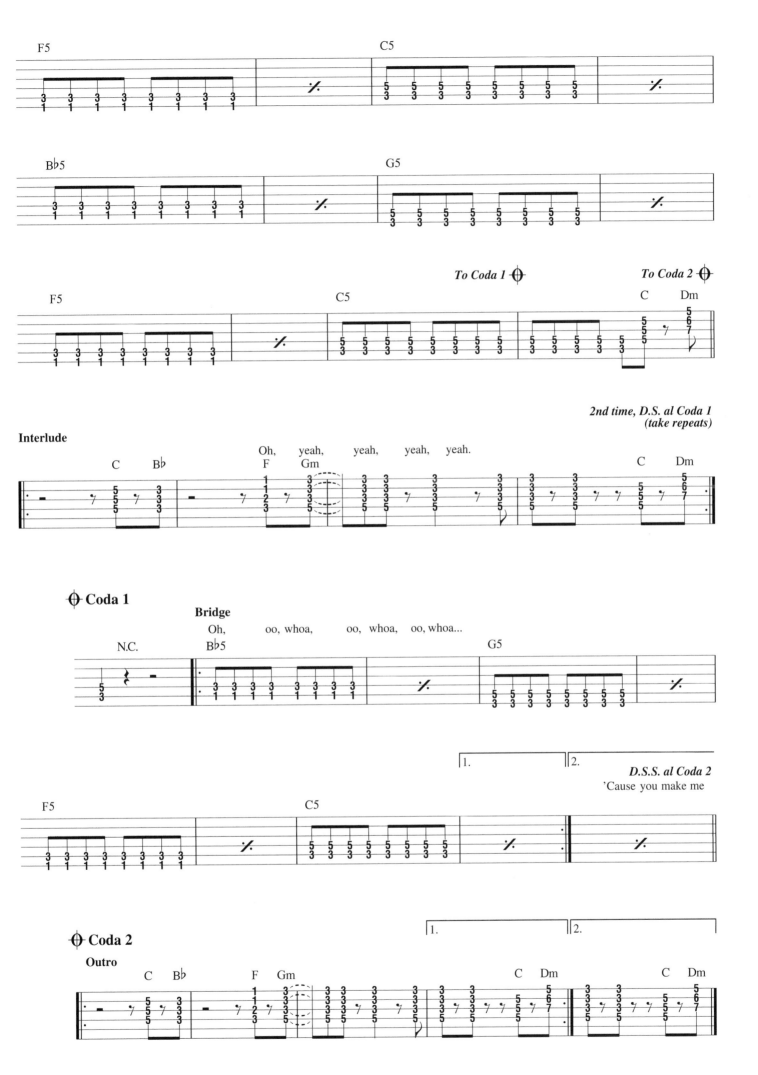

Keyboard

Locked Out of Heaven

Words and Music by Bruno Mars, Ari Levine and Philip Lawrence

Interlude

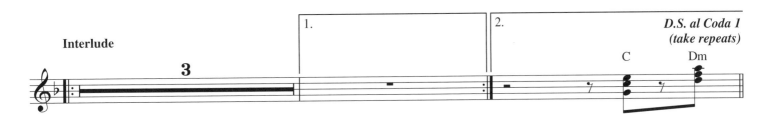

⊕ **Coda 1**

Bridge

Oh,   oo, whoa,   oo, whoa,   oo, whoa...

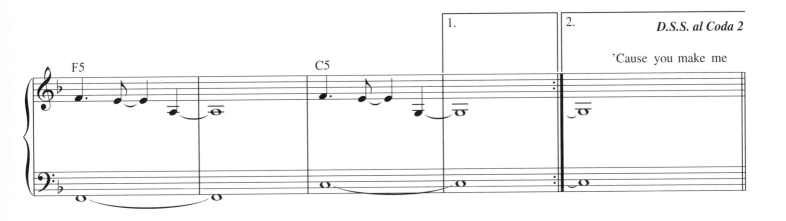

⊕ **Coda 2**
Outro

Play one octave lower

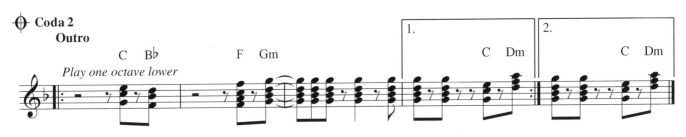

Locked Out of Heaven

Words and Music by Bruno Mars, Ari Levine and Philip Lawrence

Key of Dm

Intro
Moderately fast ♩ = 144

 Verse

1. Nev - er had much faith...
2. You bring me to my knees...

4.

Pre-Chorus
'Cause your sex takes me to par - a - dise...

'Cause you make me

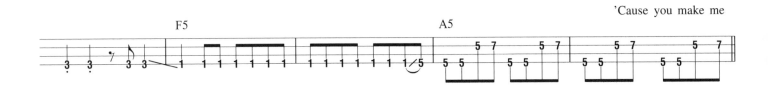

Chorus
feel like...

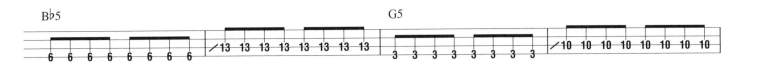

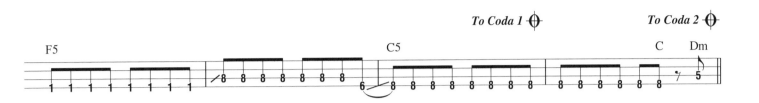

To Coda 1 ⊕   *To Coda 2* ⊕

2nd time, D.S. al Coda 1
(take repeats)

Interlude

Oh   yeah,   yeah, yeah, yeah...

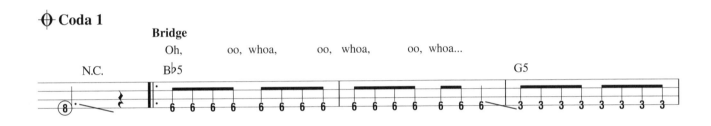

⊕ **Coda 1**

Bridge

Oh,   oo, whoa,   oo, whoa,   oo, whoa...

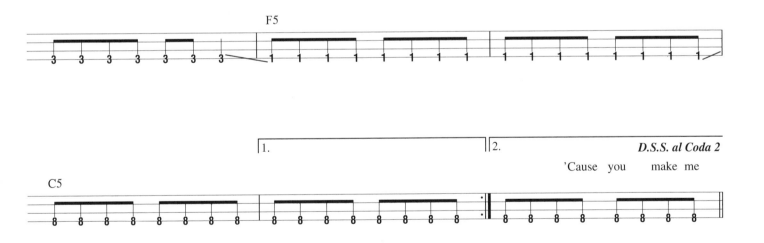

D.S.S. al Coda 2

'Cause you   make me

⊕ **Coda 2**

Outro

Drums

Locked Out of Heaven

Words and Music by Bruno Mars, Ari Levine and Philip Lawrence

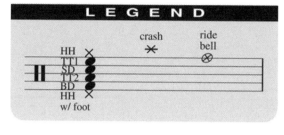

Intro
Moderately fast ♩ = 144

Verse

1. Nev - er had much   faith...

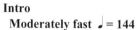

1., 2., 3.   4.

'Cause your sex

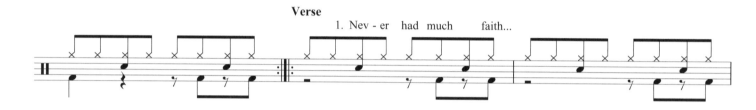

𝄋 Pre-Chorus

takes   me   to   par - a - dise...

Play 5 times

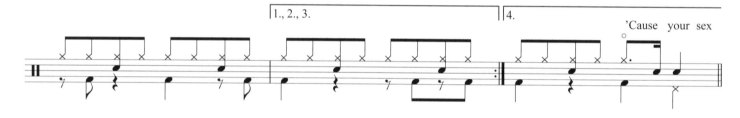

Chorus

'Cause you   make me   feel   like..

Play 7 times

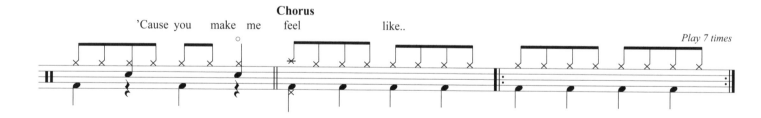

Play 4 times

To Coda ⊕

Vocal

Radioactive

Words and Music by Daniel Reynolds, Benjamin McKee, Daniel Sermon, Alexander Grant and Josh Mosser

Intro
Slow ♩ = 68

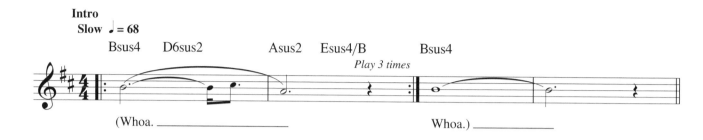

(Whoa. _____ Whoa.) _____

Verse

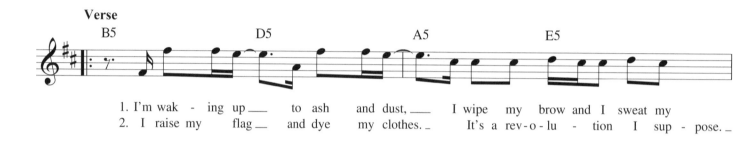

1. I'm wak - ing up ___ to ash and dust, ___ I wipe my brow and I sweat my
2. I raise my flag ___ and dye my clothes. ___ It's a rev-o-lu - tion I sup-pose. _

rust. I'm breath - ing in ___ the chem-i-cals. ___ *Inhale:* *Exhale:* Ah!
___ We're paint - ed red ___ to fit right in, ___ whoa. _

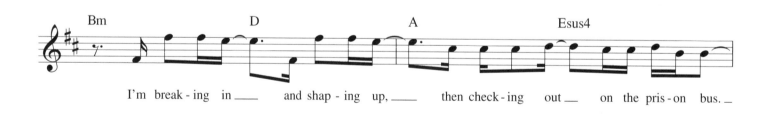

I'm break-ing in ___ and shap-ing up, ___ then check-ing out ___ on the pris-on bus.

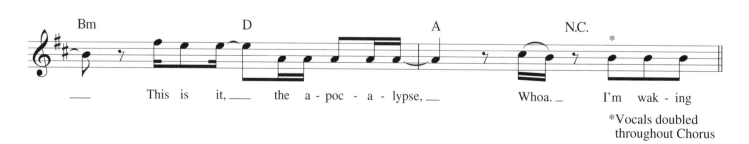

___ This is it, ___ the a-poc-a-lypse, ___ Whoa. _ I'm wak - ing

*Vocals doubled
throughout Chorus

Chorus

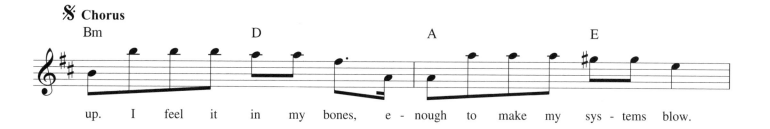

up. I feel it in my bones, e - nough to make my sys - tems blow.

Wel - come to the new age, to the new age. Wel - come to the new age, ___ to the new age. __

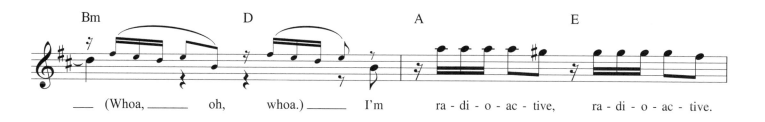

__ (Whoa, _____ oh, whoa.) _____ I'm ra - di - o - ac - tive, ra - di - o - ac - tive.

To Coda

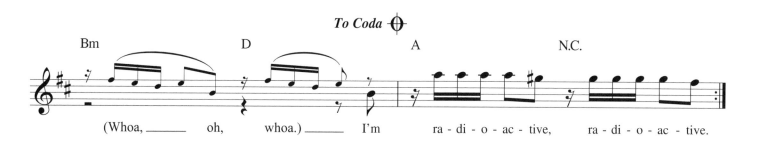

(Whoa, _____ oh, whoa.) _____ I'm ra - di - o - ac - tive, ra - di - o - ac - tive.

Bridge

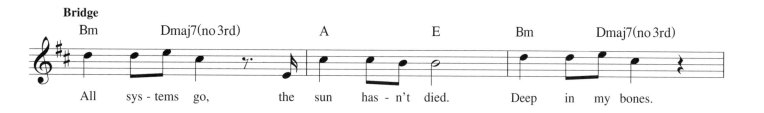

All sys - tems go, the sun has - n't died. Deep in my bones.

D.S. al Coda ⊕ **Coda**

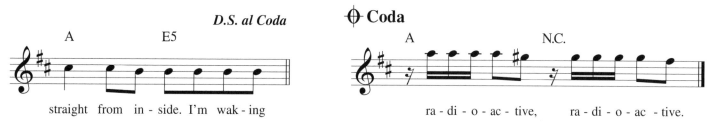

straight from in - side. I'm wak - ing ra - di - o - ac - tive, ra - di - o - ac - tive.

Guitar

Radioactive

Words and Music by Daniel Reynolds, Benjamin McKee, Daniel Sermon, Alexander Grant and Josh Mosser

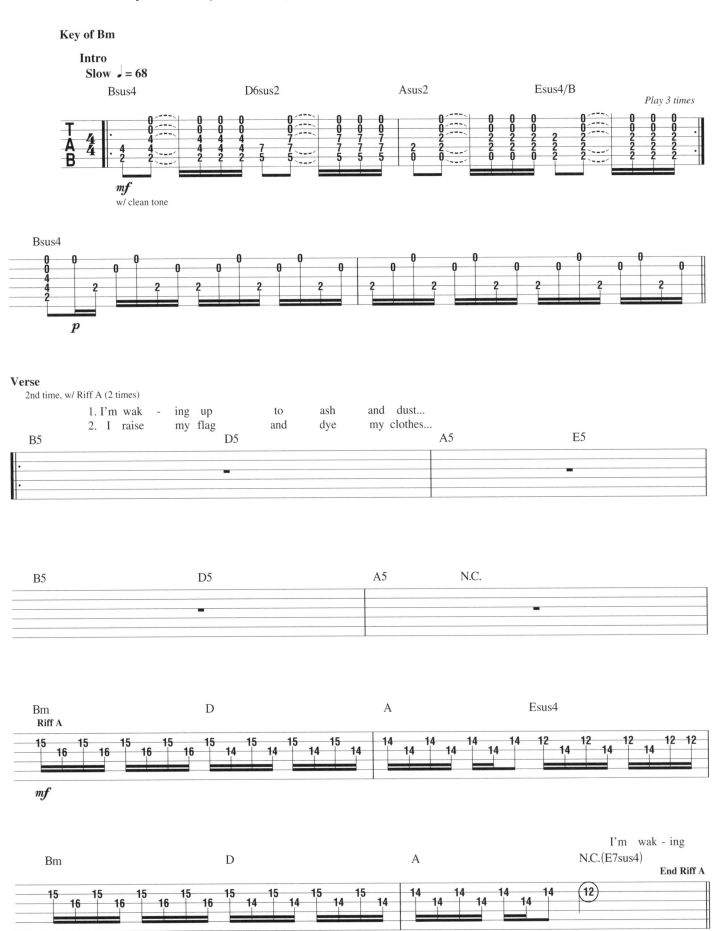

Chorus

up.   I   feel   it   in   my   bones...

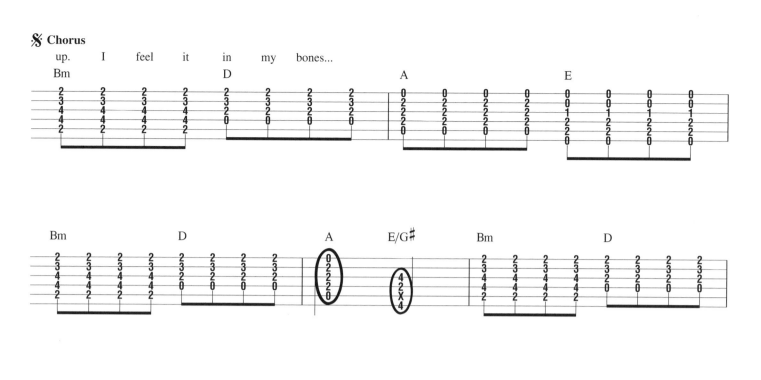

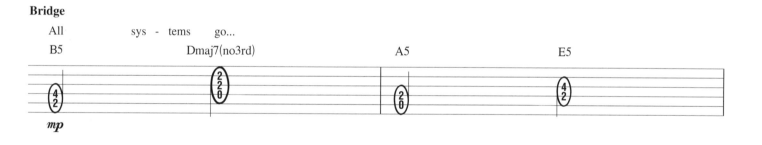

To Coda ⊕

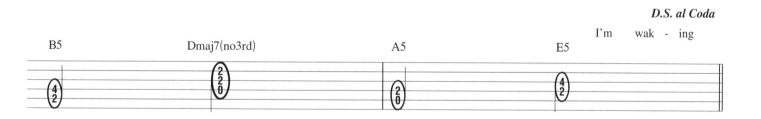

Bridge

All   sys - tems   go...

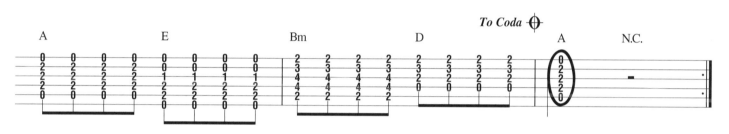

mp

D.S. al Coda

I'm   wak - ing

⊕ Coda

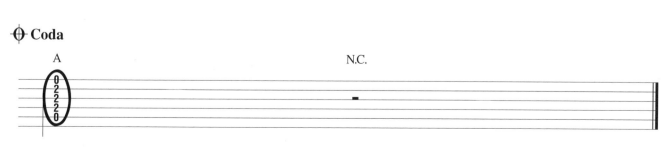

Keyboard

Radioactive

Words and Music by Daniel Reynolds, Benjamin McKee, Daniel Sermon, Alexander Grant and Josh Mosser

Verse
1. I'm wak - ing up   to ash and dust...
2. I raise my flag   and dye my clothes...

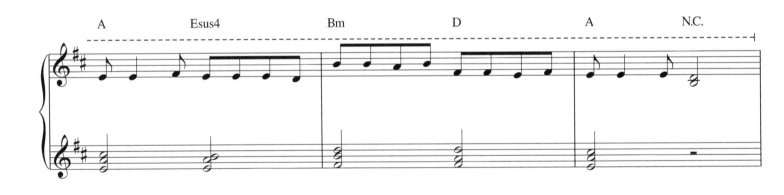

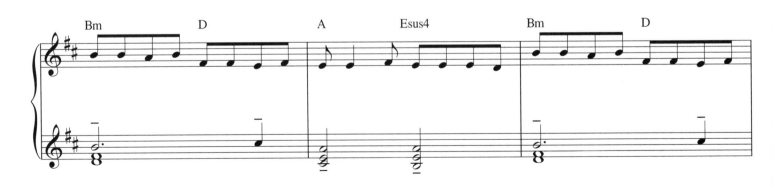

Bass

Radioactive

Words and Music by Daniel Reynolds, Benjamin McKee, Daniel Sermon, Alexander Grant and Josh Mosser

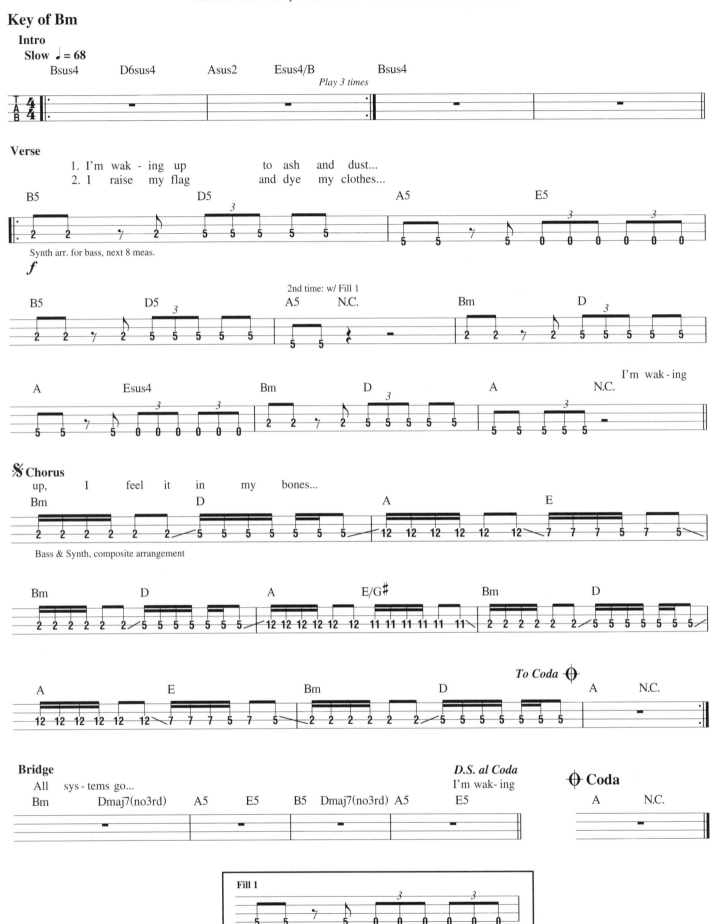

Drums

Radioactive

Words and Music by Daniel Reynolds, Benjamin McKee, Daniel Sermon, Alexander Grant and Josh Mosser

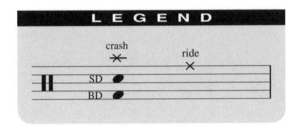

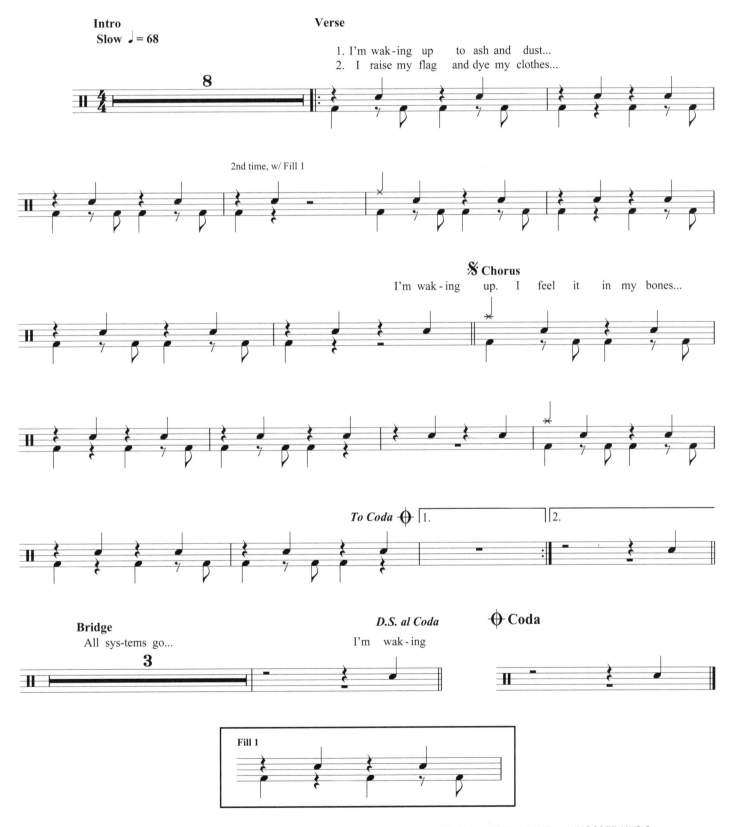

Vocal

Some Nights

Words and Music by Jeff Bhasker, Andrew Dost, Jack Antonoff and Nate Ruess

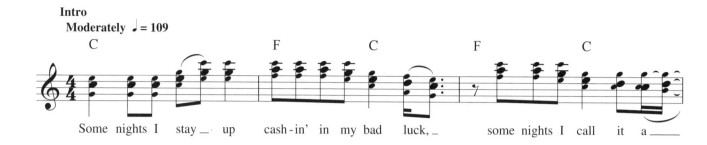

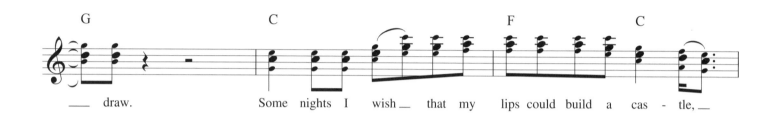

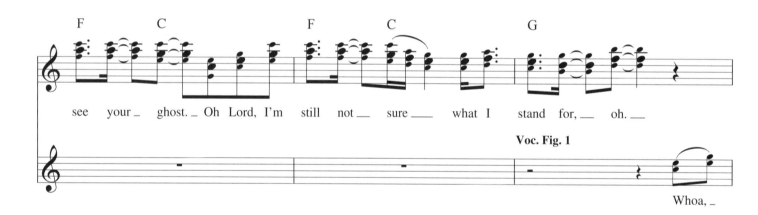

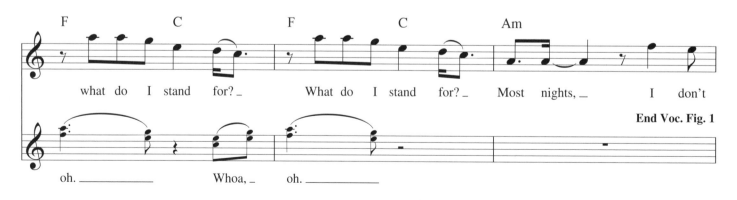

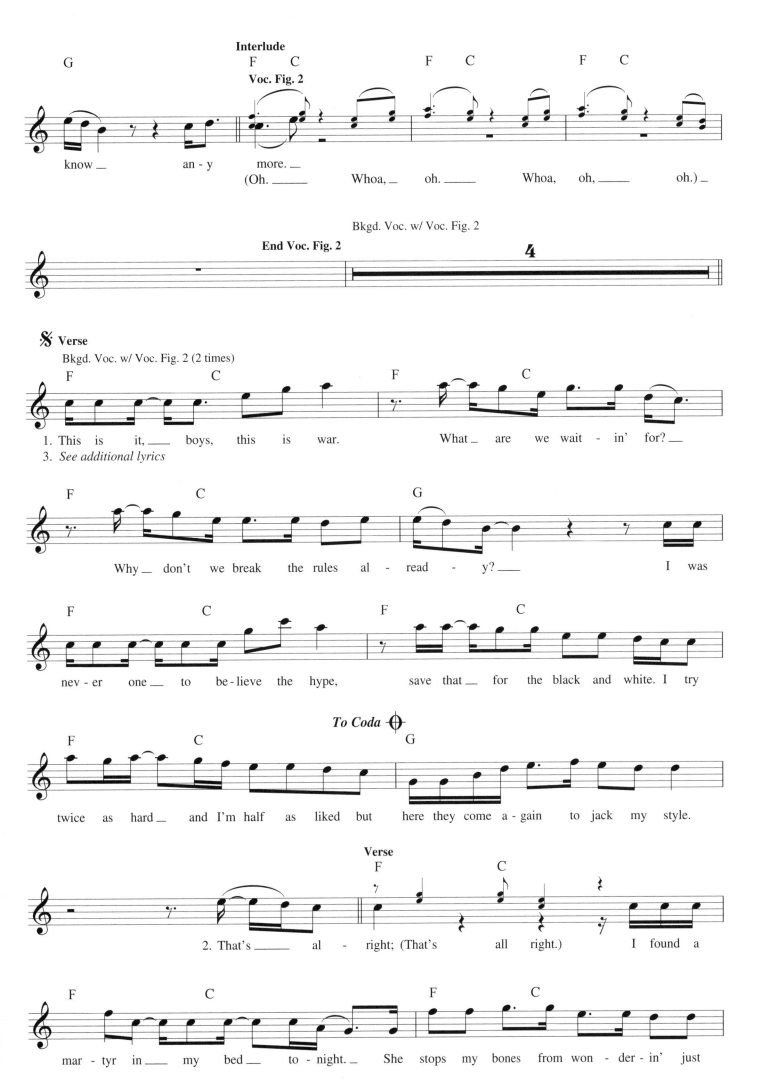

31

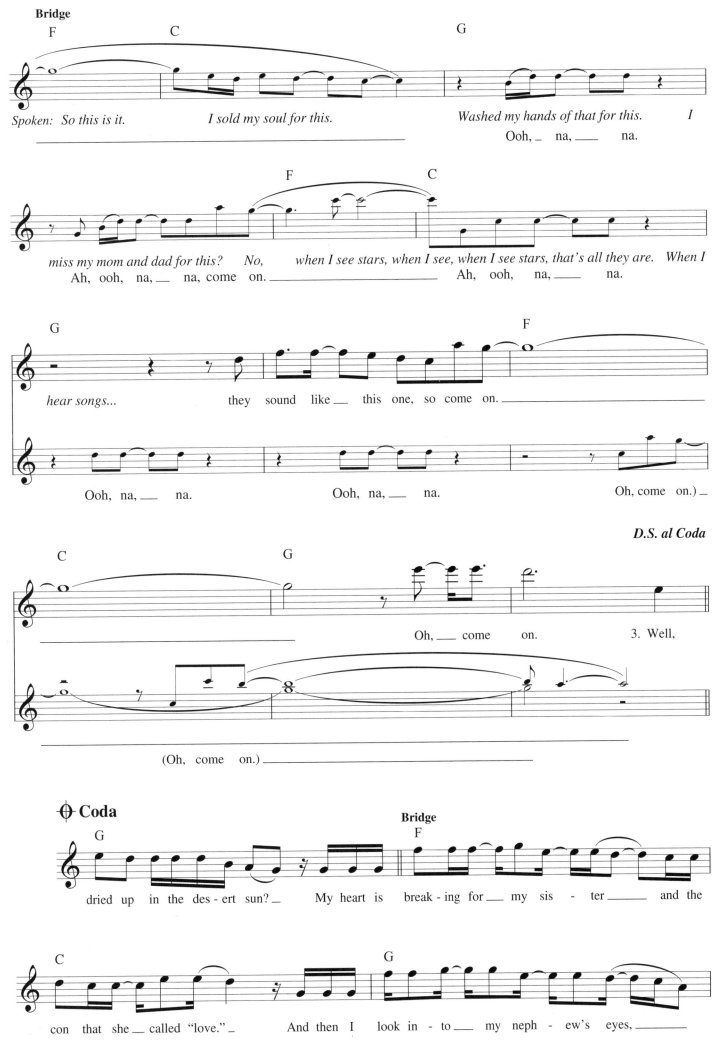

man, you would-n't be - lieve ___ the most a - maz - ing things

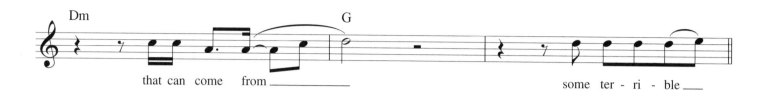

that can come from _____ some ter - ri - ble ___

Interlude

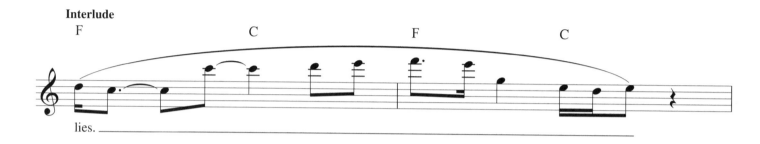

lies. ___

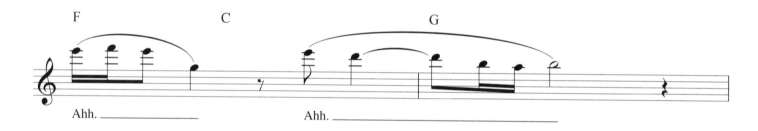

Ahh. ___ Ahh. ___

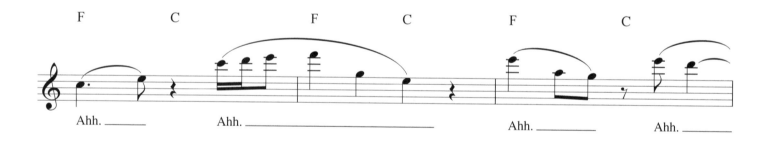

Ahh. ___ Ahh. ___ Ahh. ___ Ahh. ___

Interlude
Bkgd. Voc. w/ Voc. Fig. 2 (2 times)

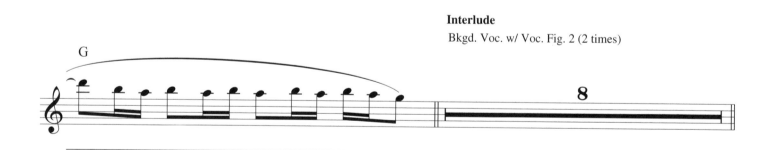

8

Outro-Verse

The oth - er night you would-n't be - lieve the dream ___ I just had a - bout ___ you and me.

34

I called you up but we both a - gree.

It's for the best you did – n't lis - ten. _____

It's for the best we get __ our dis - tance, __ oh. _____

Bkgd. Voc. w/ Voc. Fig. 2 (2 times)

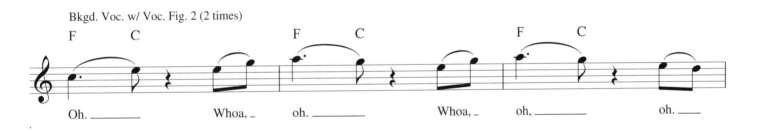

Oh. _____ Whoa, _ oh. _____ Whoa, _ oh, _____ oh. ___

Additional Lyrics

3. Well, that is it, guys, that is all.
   Five minutes in and I'm bored again.
   Ten years of this, I'm not sure if anybody understands.
   This one is not for the folks at home.
   Sorry to leave, Mom, I had to go.
   Who the (fuck) wants to die alone
   All dried up in the desert sun?

Guitar

Some Nights

Words and Music by Jeff Bhasker, Andrew Dost, Jack Antonoff and Nate Ruess

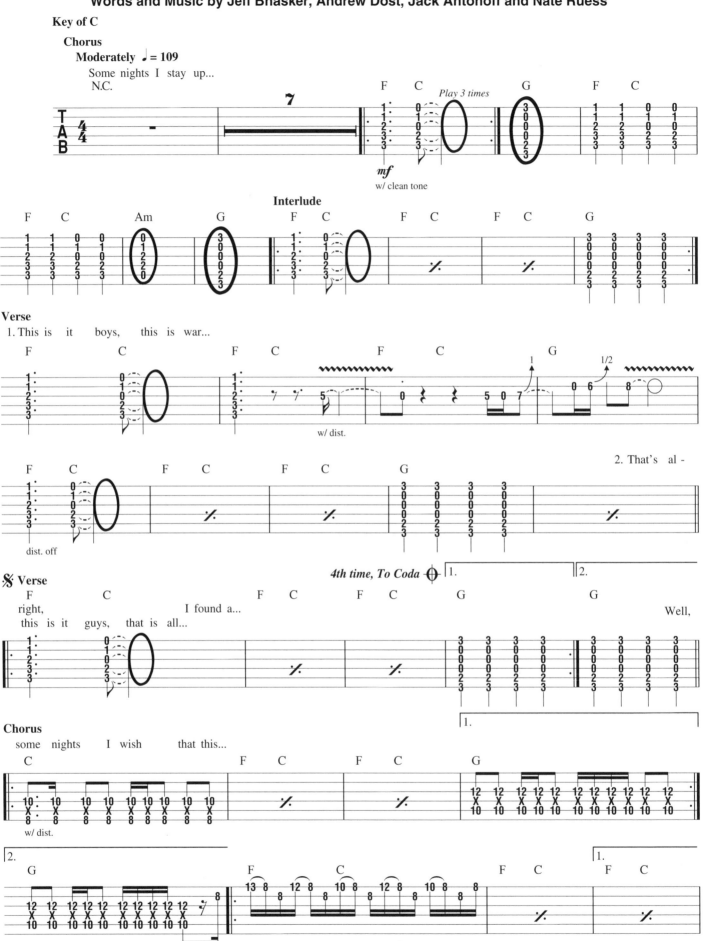

36

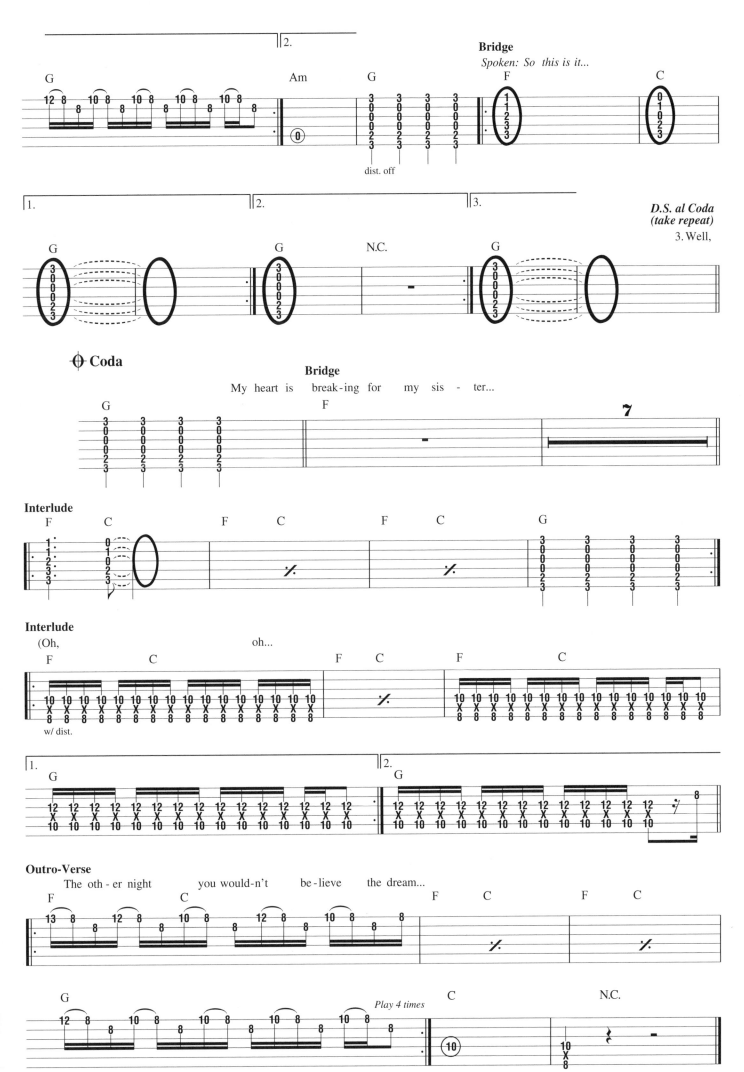

Keyboard

Some Nights

Words and Music by Jeff Bhasker, Andrew Dost, Jack Antonoff and Nate Ruess

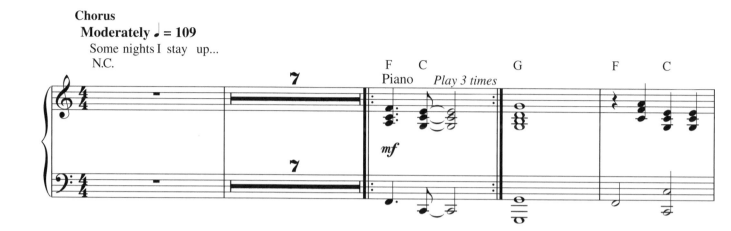

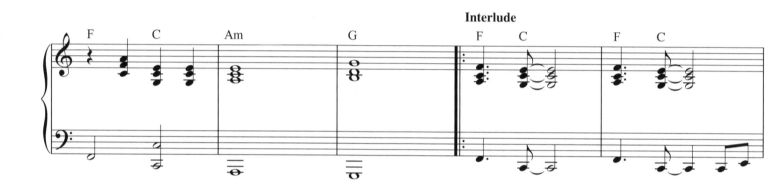

Bridge

Spoken: So this is it.

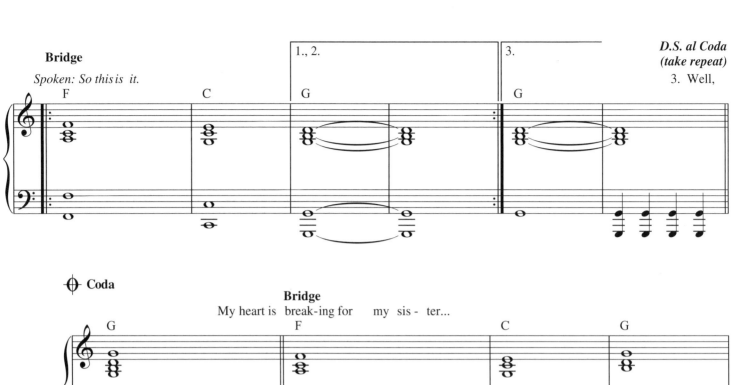

1., 2.

3.

D.S. al Coda
(take repeat)
3. Well,

Coda

Bridge
My heart is break-ing for   my sis - ter...

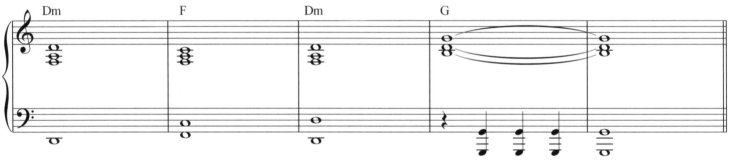

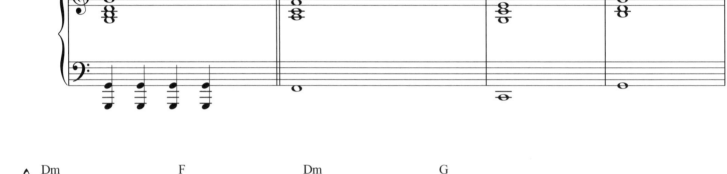

Interlude

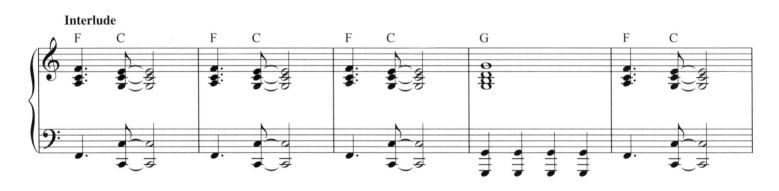

Interlude
(Oh,   oh...

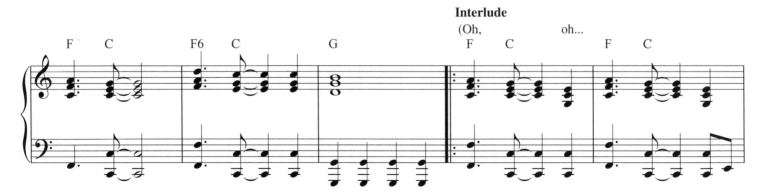

40

Outro-Verse

The oth-er night   you would-n't be-lieve the dream...

Bass

Some Nights

Words and Music by Jeff Bhasker, Andrew Dost, Jack Antonoff and Nate Ruess

Key of C

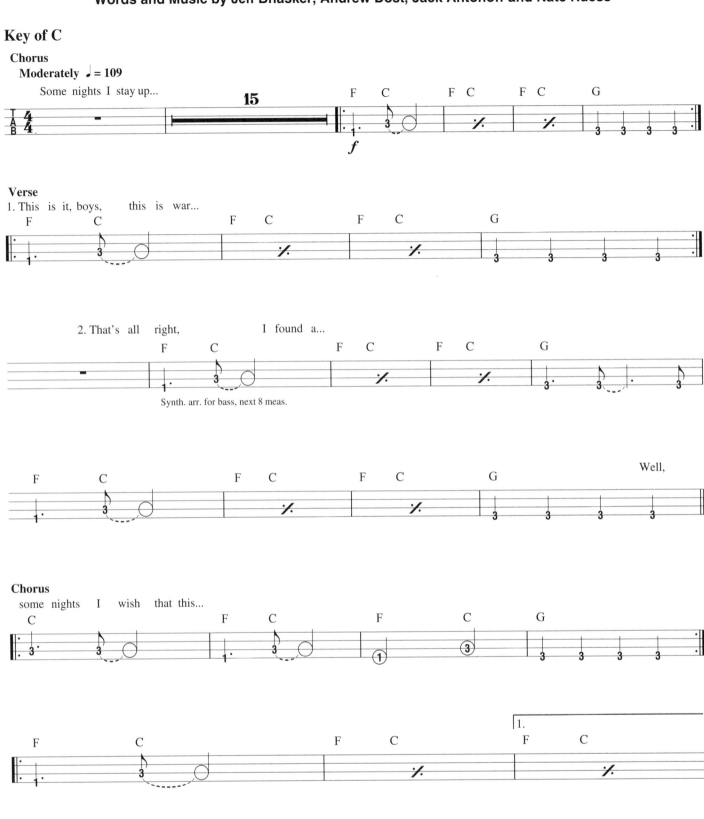

Bridge

Spoken: So this is it...

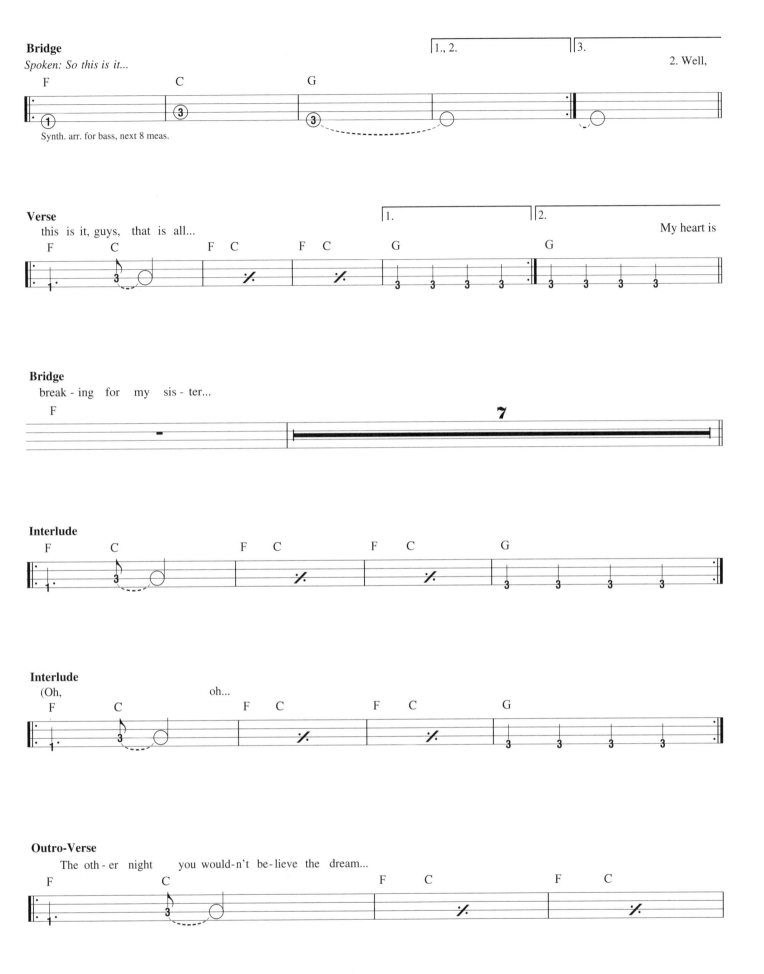

Synth. arr. for bass, next 8 meas.

Verse

this is it, guys, that is all...

Bridge

break - ing for my sis - ter...

Interlude

Interlude

(Oh, oh...

Outro-Verse

The oth - er night you would-n't be - lieve the dream...

Play 4 times

Drums

Some Nights

Words and Music by Jeff Bhasker, Andrew Dost, Jack Antonoff and Nate Ruess

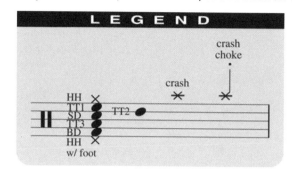

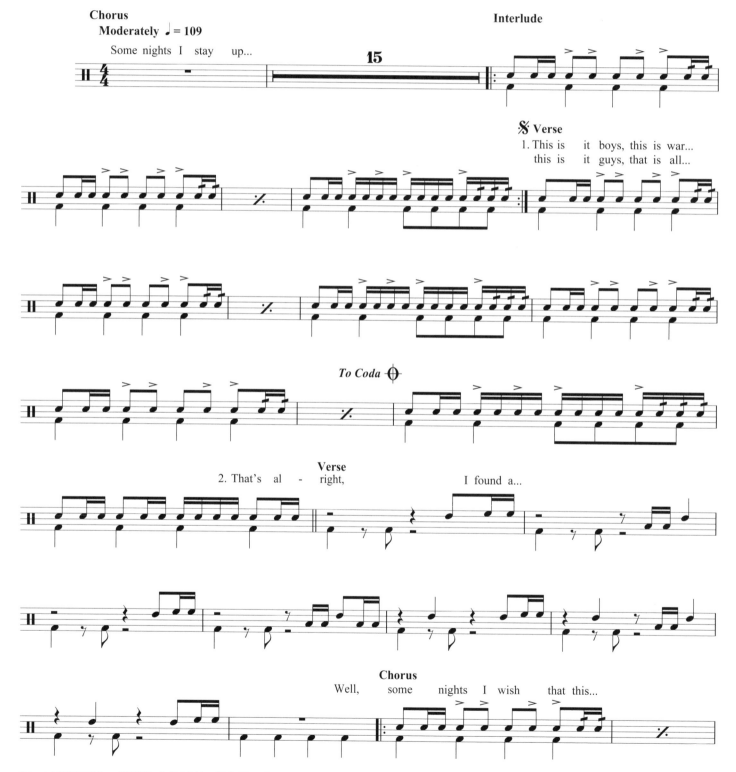

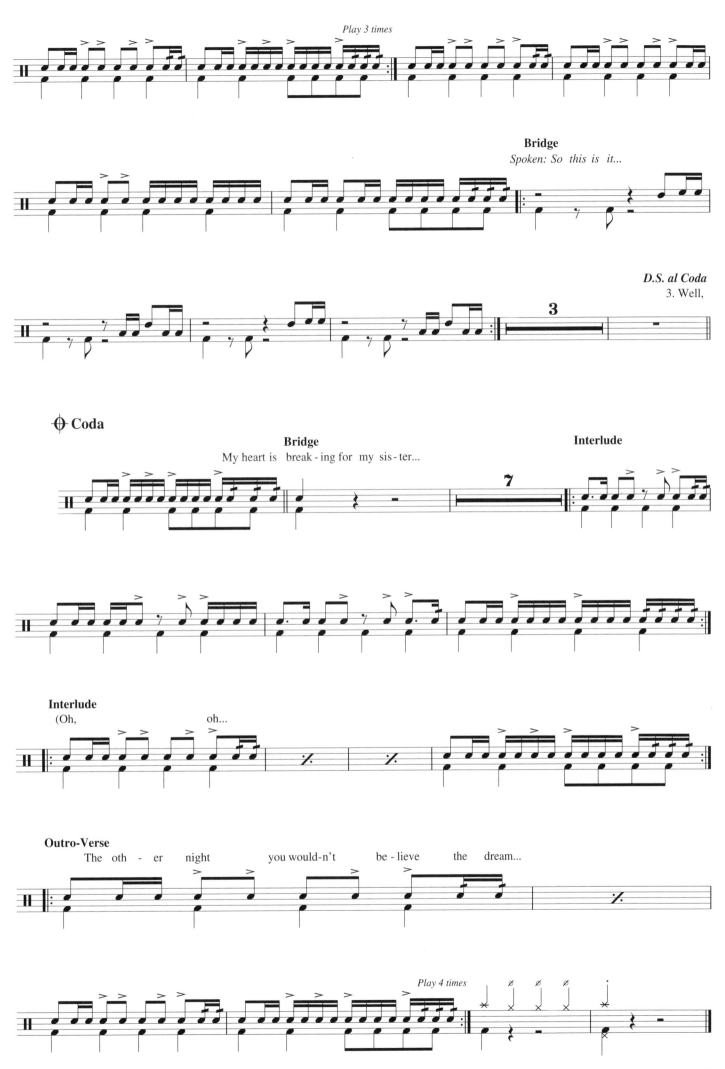

Vocal

Too Close

Words and Music by Alex Claire and Jim Duguid

Too Close

Words and Music by Alex Claire and Jim Duguid

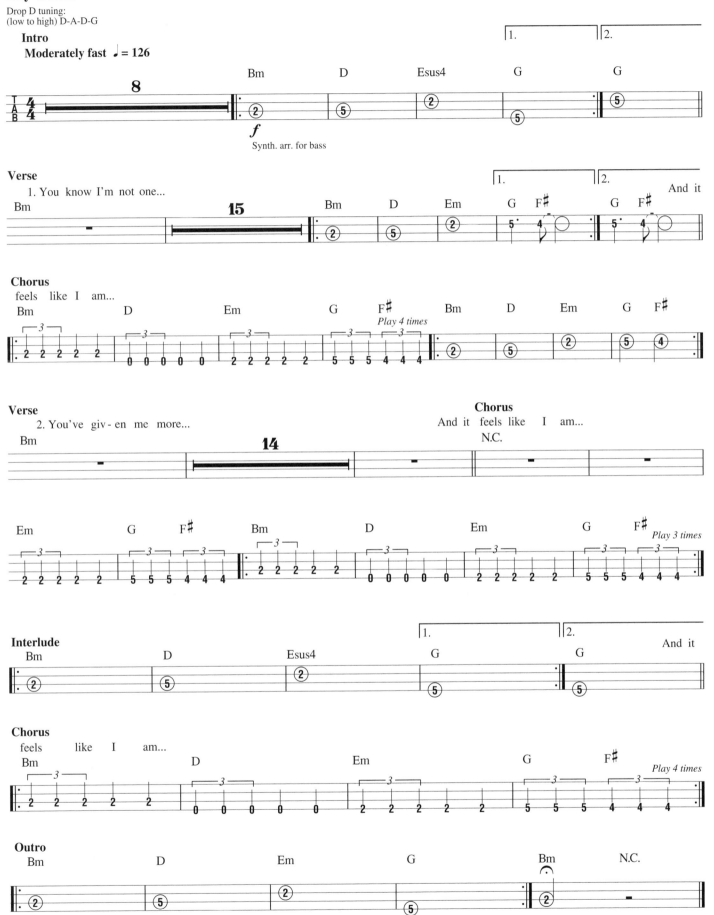

Guitar

Too Close

Words and Music by Alex Claire and Jim Duguid

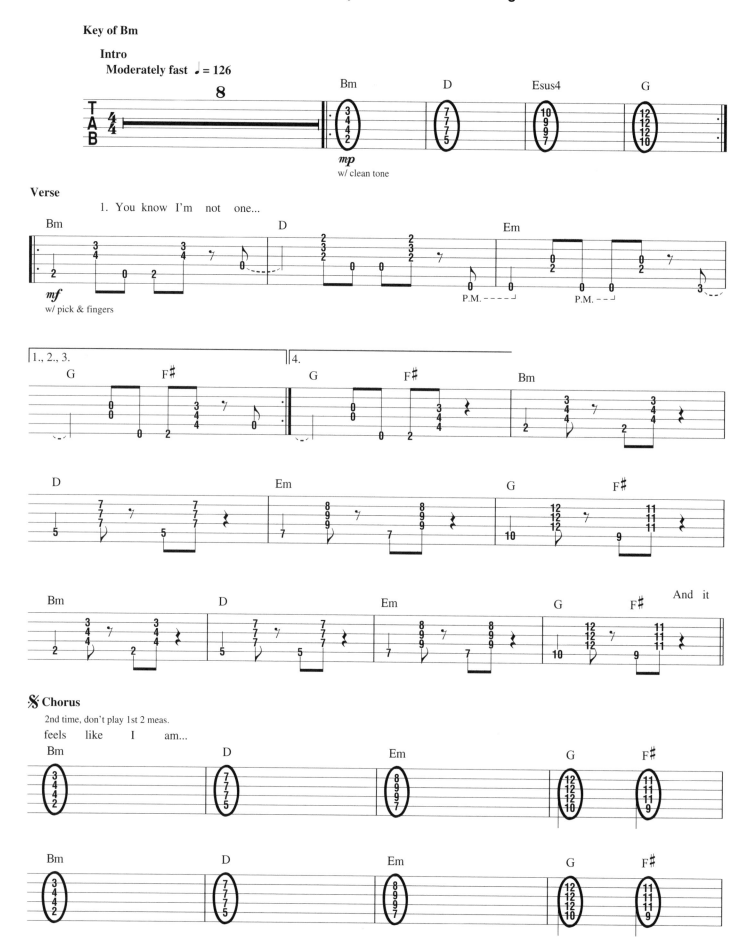

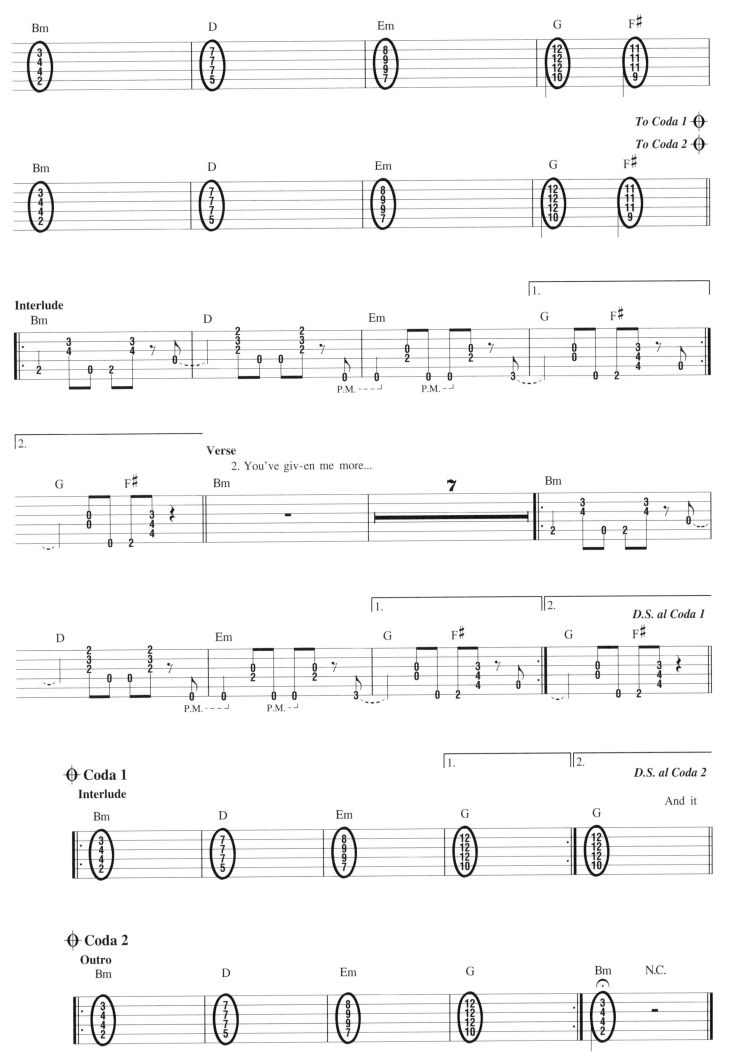

Keyboard

Too Close
Words and Music by Alex Claire and Jim Duguid

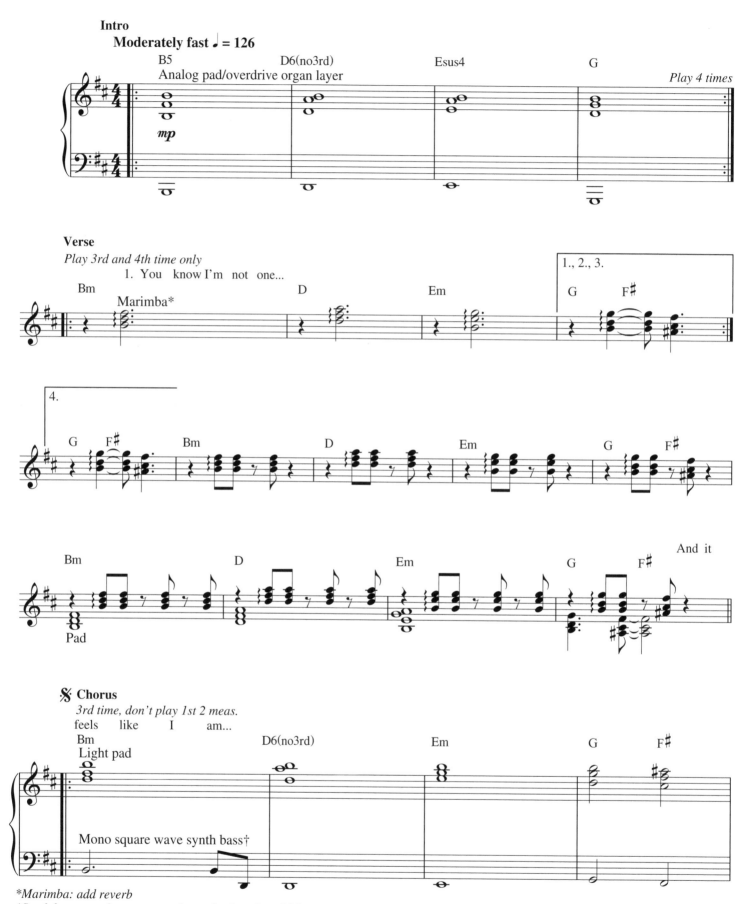

Intro
Moderately fast ♩ = 126

*Marimba: add reverb
†Synth bass sound, programmed to pulse in a dotted 8th note rhythm.

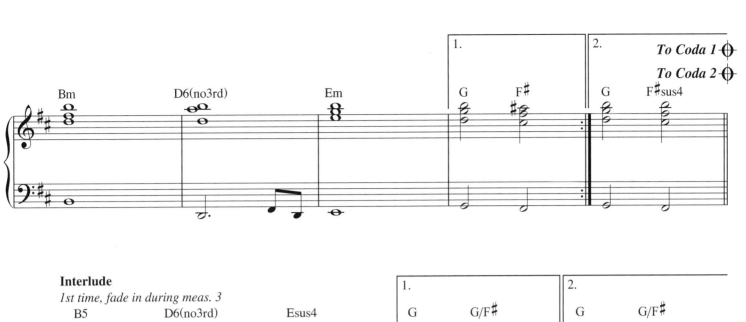

Interlude

1st time, fade in during meas. 3

Pad (both hands)

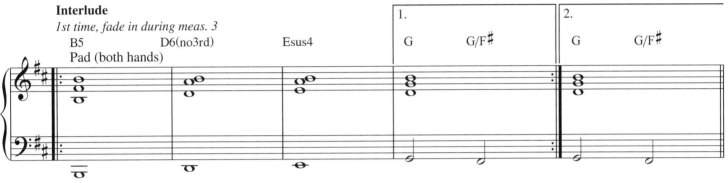

Verse

2. You've giv-en me more...

Light pad

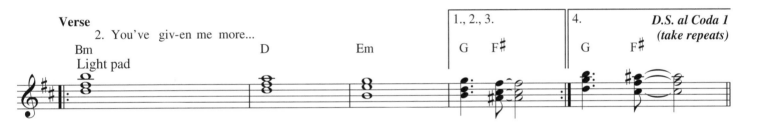

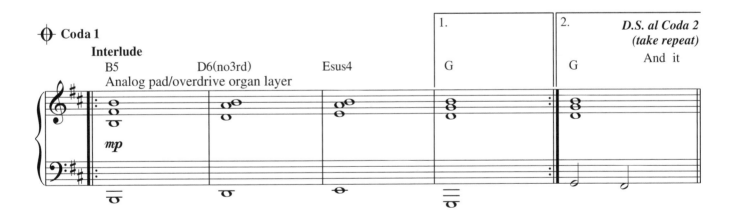

⊕ Coda 1

Interlude

Analog pad/overdrive organ layer

mp

⊕ Coda 2

Outro

Analog pad/overdrive organ layer

mp

cresc. on repeat

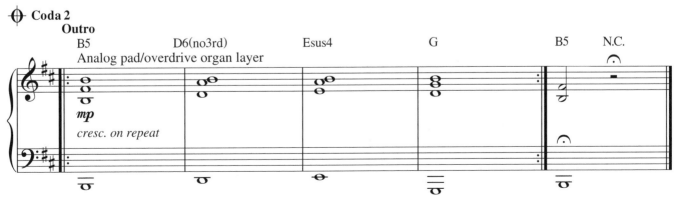

Drums

Too Close

Words and Music by Alex Claire and Jim Duguid

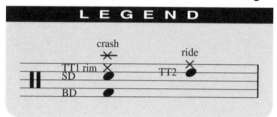

feels   like   I   am...

Coda

Interlude

Chorus

And it   feels   like   I   am...

Play 4 times

Play 3 times

Outro

PERFORMANCE TIPS

HOME

VOCAL

- Sing Verse 1 with an intimate character. Sing stronger on Verses 2 & 3.
- When singing sustained diphthong vowels, sustain the more open vowel sound (e.g. "down" should be sung "*da*-oon," and "wave" should be sung "*weh*-eev"); in general, avoid raising the back of the tongue when sustaining vowel sounds.
- On the Chorus, vocals are sung softly the first time only.
- Reminder: after Verse 2, the Chorus is sung 3 times in a row. After Verse 3, the Chorus is sung 2 times. Then go to the Outro.

GUITAR

- For the Intro and Verse 1, rock your pick back and forth between strings 5 and 4 and use your second and/or third finger for strings 3 and 2.
- When the strumming starts (Verse 2), slightly accent the "and" of beats 1 and 3.
- In the Chorus, play the G chord with your ring finger on string 6 (allowing it to dampen string 5) and your pinky on string 1. Then you can add your index to string 2, fret 1 for Gsus4.

KEYBOARD

- Split keyboard, or use a separate keyboard for accordion sound, in order to make a smooth transition to accordion at the 5th ending.
- Use organ as a pad: Hammond B3 with no vibrato, slow rotary speaker
- Do not overbalance organ or accordion to band. Play these sounds at the softest volume possible to fill out the overall sound.
- Use bell/string pad to supplement vocals during chorus. Keep this sound fairly prominent in the mix.
- To subtly shape pad and accordion sounds while sustaining, use a volume pedal. Do not apply volume pedal to bell/ strings sound.

BASS

- Dial in a dull, bottom-heavy tone, and pluck either with your thumb or a pick, sounding the strings near the fingerboard. The goal is to achieve a warm, round sound not unlike that of an upright bass.
- Lock in tightly with the drums, and allow a bit of space between each note.
- Stick to the quarter-note pulse of the song; avoid embellishing. There's a lot going on with the guitars and harmony vocals, so it's best to lay back and stay out of the way. Less is definitely more in this case.

DRUMS

- Drums enter with quarter note bass drum to set up the groove.
- The main groove is modified to follow the live drummer's adaptation played as a "train beat".
- The only fills are accent variations of the snare groove. Keep it simple.

LOCKED OUT OF HEAVEN

VOCAL

- Many of the syncopated phrases in the Verses and Pre-Chorus are sung with staccato articulation—disconnected from one word to the next.

- In the Verses, "night" is sung "nigh, I, ight," and "stay" is sung "stay, ay, ay."

- In the Chorus, "long" is sung "la, oo, ah, oo, ong."

- In the Pre-Chorus, make sure lead and background vocals articulate the lyrics exactly the same way and are perfectly in sync ("...me to par-a..." should be sung staccato).

GUITAR

- Pay attention to the rests in the Intro and Verses, and keep those chord strums short and staccato. Listen to the hi-hat and concentrate on really locking in with the time.

- For the Chorus, dig in (pick harder) a bit and feel free to kick on just a little bit of distortion (not much though).

- All downstrokes will sound best in the Chorus.

KEYBOARD

- During Intro and Verse, match your note length with guitar note length, to make rhythm sound clean.

- Use highly resonant mono Analog Lead and Synth bass sounds.

- For analog lead portamento (port.), written rhythms and pitches are approximate: Note should slide upward for the full duration of each measure.

- Use a sawtooth wave "Synth lead" sound which contains both the written pitch and the pitch an octave higher.

- Synth lead sound should be prominent in the "mix."

BASS

- The intro hits (in the pickup at the beginning of the song) are played with the band on the "ands" of beats 3 and 4.

- The song's signature riff is established in the first four bars.

- Make the octave figures in the two measures preceding the chorus stand out.

- Dig in hard and play strongly on the choruses.

- Hang onto the downward slide that starts Coda 1 and play it for its full duration.

DRUMS

- Count off the song so the band starts together with bass drum pickups on the and of beat 3.

- Play the four measure main groove exactly since the syncopated bass drum follows the band "hits".

- Keep the Pre-Chorus and Chorus simple and driving.

- Note the half-time feel in the final Chorus.

- The songs ends abruptly with the band on the and of 4.

RADIOACTIVE

VOCAL

- Sing strong throughout, except the Bridge should be a little softer
- In the Verses, intensify some plosive consonants to achieve a tough-guy style ("chemicals," "prison bus," "apocalypse").
- Sing with a relaxed tempo, slightly behind the beat.
- If applicable, have sound tech add desired vocal sound effects to the mix for the singing of "radioactive, radioactive," during the Chorus. (The recording has a sound effect with these lyrics sung at a constant pitch of B1 and doubled 8va).

GUITAR

- In the Intro, keep your fingers arched to make sure strings 2 and 1 ring out.
- You can keep your ring and pinky fingers on strings 4 and 3, respectively, for the whole Intro, including the Asus2. This will make the chord transitions smoother.
- Begin Riff A in 14th position with your second finger on string 2, fret 15. This way, you won't have to shift down until the Esus4 chord.
- Fret the E/G♯ chord in the chorus with your ring finger on string 6 (allowing it to dampen string 5), index on string 4, and pinky on string 3.

KEYBOARD

- Split your primary keyboard in three sections. Upper: guitar patch. Middle: Choral pad(s). Lower: Synth string pad.
- Use a secondary keyboard for Analog mono lead.
- Use slow portamento (port.) for Analog mono sound, leading into verse 1. Note should slide upward for the full two-measures.
- Play Light choral pad sound at a low level in the mix. If possible, use a heavier choral pad sound during bridge.
- During chorus, use a full, big sounding Synth string pad in the left hand.
- Bridge is suddenly softer. Lessen volume accordingly, but play the line with authority.

BASS

- To emulate the synth bass sound heard on the recording, use a distortion pedal.
- This song should be played heavily throughout. Dig into each rhythm and be careful not to rush, especially the triplets.
- Note that the chorus is played entirely on the A string.
- The fourth measure of the 1st verse contains a break after the first beat, whereas the fourth measure of the 2nd verse does not.

DRUMS

- The drums enter at the first verse.
- If possible, play on an electronic drum kit or trigger drum samples to emulate the "big" bass and snare drum sounds like the recording.
- Keep it simple like the drum sequence on the original recording.

SOME NIGHTS

VOCAL

- In the Intro and Chorus, take care that all singers take breaths and end phrases together.
- On "still wake *up*," the *p* is pronounced on the and of beat 3.
- On "still not sure," take a breath on the and of beat 3.
- Make sure to end together on "friends for a *change*.")
- Use grit on certain words and phrases ("*this is war*" "*why* don't we break")
- In the Interlude, use falsetto. If applicable, have sound tech run lead vocal through a pitch-correction processor for this section only. Processor should be set to a C major scale and a quick correction speed.

GUITAR

- Use either a two-channel amp with one channel set clean and the other distorted, or use a clean amp with a distortion pedal.
- For the octave shapes, such as in the Chorus and Interlude, use your index finger to dampen the in-between string to keep it quiet and allow it to lay flat and mute the higher strings as well.

KEYBOARD

- Try to play all notes of each chord *exactly* together.
- When piano enters (measure 9), concentrate on keeping tempo and eighth note subdivision even and consistent.
- At verse 2, dynamic level drops suddenly to *mp*. Make this dynamic change clearly, with your playing (not with keyboard's volume control) *on*, not after, beat 1 of that measure.
- When changing dynamics, do not let the tempo budge.
- Whole notes on bridge should also be played exactly in time. Do not roll chords.

BASS

- Simplicity is king; hold down the bottom end and the song's harmonic rhythm while keeping solid time, and allow the band and vocals to work off of your foundation.
- Dial in a bass-heavy tone and roll back the highs, especially to emulate the synth bass sound heard on the recording.
- Don't just play the notes; use dynamics throughout to make the song come alive. Come in strong on the intro chorus, then back off a bit for the 1st verse, come down even more for the 2nd verse, then build back up for the following chorus.

DRUMS

- Drums enter at the interlude with a "marching" type snare groove.
- On the 2nd verse and Bridge, play the written tom part on an electronic drum kit to emulate the sound samples of the original recording.
- For the ending, use the hi-hat for timing to cue the abrupt ending cut with the band.

TOO CLOSE

VOCAL

- Come in on the and of beat 2 after you hear the clean electric guitar starting picking the broken Bm chord.
- Sing medium strong with clean tone throughout.
- Decorate long, sustained vowels by rearticulating them on a change of pitch (e.g. "heading sep'rate *way-ays,*" and "can really *say, ay.*"
- The 2nd time through the Chorus, the lead vocal sings a cappella for two measures.
- In the Chorus, use grace note slides to approach *"feels like I am just too."*

GUITAR

- The Verse can be played with pick and fingers or with fingers only. Try both to see what feels better.
- Even though you're only plucking certain strings in the verse, it's best to fret the whole chord if possible.
- In the Chorus, try kicking on a modulation pedal of some kind if you have it—tremolo, vibrato, phaser, etc.—to emulate the throbbing synth sound.

KEYBOARD

- Use volume pedal to crescendo throughout Intro and Interludes.
- Select an Analog pad whose resonance increases throughout the eight bars of the Intro and Interludes.
- During Choruses, use a light, airy pad sound in the right hand; use a heavy, powerful Mono synth bass in the left hand.
- Observe the sudden dynamic drop to mp for Interludes and Outro.
- Use the same pad for Verse 2 as for the Chorus.
- Suggested keyboard setup:
    Keyboard I:
        First patch: Split keyboard, with Marimba above the split point and Analog pad/Organ below split point.
        Second patch: Light pad
    Keyboard II: Mono square wave synth bass.

BASS

- The bass line is actually performed on a synth throughout; you may want to use a light distortion effect on the choruses to emulate the sound.
- The bass is tuned to drop-D to accommodate the low synth notes; don't forget that all pitches on the E string (now tuned down one whole step to D) are played two frets higher than in standard tuning.
- Be sure not to rush the quarter-note triplets in the choruses.
- The verses should be played softer than the choruses. Use dynamics between these sections to build tension.

DRUMS

- Song begins with keyboard. Drums enter on measure 9.
- Play the main groove on the tom rim.
- Keep the beginning of the Chorus simple with the bass and snare drum part, then add the "rim" part the 2nd half.
- Play the Outro on the tom rim only (no bass drum).

CD INDEX

CD 1

TITLE	FORMAT	TRACK
Home	Full Demo	1
Locked Out of Heaven	Full Demo	2
Radioactive	Full Demo	3
Some Nights	Full Demo	4
Too Close	Full Demo	5
Home	Vocal Sing Along	6
Locked Out of Heaven	Vocal Sing Along	7
Radioactive	Vocal Sing Along	8
Some Nights	Vocal Sing Along	9
Too Close	Vocal Sing Along	10
Home	Drum Play Along	11
Locked Out of Heaven	Drum Play Along	12
Radioactive	Drum Play Along	13
Some Nights	Drum Play Along	14
Too Close	Drum Play Along	15

CD 2

Home	Guitar Play Along	1
Locked Out of Heaven	Guitar Play Along	2
Radioactive	Guitar Play Along	3
Some Nights	Guitar Play Along	4
Too Close	Guitar Play Along	5
Home	Keyboard Play Along	6
Locked Out of Heaven	Keyboard Play Along	7
Radioactive	Keyboard Play Along	8
Some Nights	Keyboard Play Along	9
Too Close	Keyboard Play Along	10
Home	Bass Play Along	11
Locked Out of Heaven	Bass Play Along	12
Radioactive	Bass Play Along	13
Some Nights	Bass Play Along	14
Too Close	Bass Play Along	15

ROCK WITH
HAL•LEONARD

ROCK BAND CAMP ALL ACCESS

These books are designed for the first-time performer or weekend warrior who's learning how to play in a band. They include parts and playing tips for the entire band: two guitars or one guitar and keyboard, bass, drums, and singer! Each book comes with two CDs that contain full-band tracks for each song as well as "minus-one" tracks for each instrument for each song so players can practice on their own between band rehearsals.

CLASSIC ROCK – VOLUME 1
Bang a Gong (Get It On) (T. Rex) • The Boys Are Back in Town (Thin Lizzy) • China Grove (Doobie Brothers) • Free Fallin' (Tom Petty) • Jet Airliner (Steve Miller Band).

Guitar/Bass/Drums/Singer
00121688.........................$14.99

TODAY'S HITS – VOLUME 2
Home (Phillip Phillips) • Locked Out of Heaven (Bruno Mars) • Radioactive (Imagine Dragons) • Some Nights (fun.) • Too Close (Alex Clare).

Guitar/Bass/Drums/Singer
00121150.........................$14.99

POP/ROCK HITS – VOLUME 3
Don't Know Why (Norah Jones) • Give Me One Reason (Tracy Chapman) • My Favorite Mistake (Sheryl Crow) • Rolling in the Deep (Adele) • White Horse (Taylor Swift).

Guitar/Bass/Keyboard/Drums/Singer
00121819.........................$14.99

ROCK HITS – VOLUME 4
Beautiful Day (U2) • Billie Jean (Michael Jackson) • Clocks (Coldplay) • It's My Life (Bon Jovi) • Smooth (Santana).

Guitar/Bass/Keyboard/Drums/Singer
00121820 ....$14.99

HAL•LEONARD®
halleonard.com

0314

Guitar Chord Songbooks

Each 6" x 9" book includes complete lyrics, chord symbols, and guitar chord diagrams.

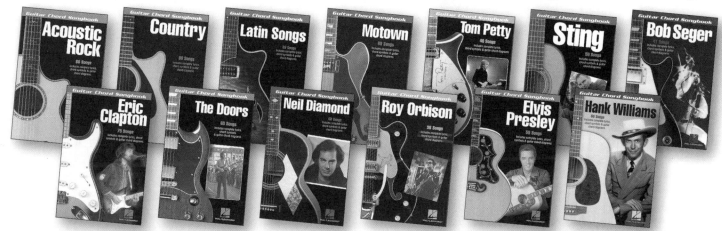

Acoustic Hits
00701787 . . . . $14.99

Acoustic Rock
00699540 . . . . $17.95

Adele
00102761 . . . . $14.99

Alabama
00699914 . . . . $14.95

The Beach Boys
00699566 . . . . $14.95

The Beatles (A-I)
00699558 . . . . $17.99

The Beatles (J-Y)
00699562 . . . . $17.99

Bluegrass
00702585 . . . . $14.99

Blues
00699733 . . . . $12.95

Broadway
00699920 . . . . $14.99

Johnny Cash
00699648 . . . . $17.99

Steven Curtis Chapman
00700702 . . . . $17.99

Children's Songs
00699539 . . . . $16.99

Christmas Carols
00699536 . . . . $12.99

Eric Clapton
00699567 . . . . $15.99

Classic Rock
00699598 . . . . $15.99

Coffeehouse Hits
00703318 . . . . $14.99

Country
00699534 . . . . $14.99

Country Favorites
00700609 . . . . $14.99

Country Standards
00700608 . . . . $12.95

Cowboy Songs
00699636 . . . . $12.95

Creedence Clearwater Revival
00701786 . . . . $12.99

Crosby, Stills & Nash
00701609 . . . . $12.99

John Denver
02501697 . . . . $14.99

Neil Diamond
00700606 . . . . $14.99

Disney
00701071 . . . . $14.99

The Doors
00699888 . . . . $15.99

The Best of Bob Dylan
14037617 . . . . $17.99

Early Rock
00699916 . . . . $14.99

Folksongs
00699541 . . . . $12.95

Folk Pop Rock
00699651 . . . . $14.95

40 Easy Strumming Songs
00115972 . . . . $14.99

Four Chord Songs
00701611 . . . . $12.99

Glee
00702501 . . . . $14.99

Gospel Hymns
00700463 . . . . $14.99

Grand Ole Opry®
00699885 . . . . $16.95

Green Day
00103074 . . . . $12.99

Guitar Chord Songbook White Pages
00702609 . . . . $29.99

Hillsong United
00700222 . . . . $12.95

Irish Songs
00701044 . . . . $14.99

Billy Joel
00699632 . . . . $15.99

Elton John
00699732 . . . . $15.99

Latin Songs
00700973 . . . . $14.99

Love Songs
00701043 . . . . $14.99

Bob Marley
00701704 . . . . $12.99

Paul McCartney
00385035 . . . . $16.95

Prices, contents, and availability subject to change without notice.

Steve Miller
00701146 . . . . $12.9●

Modern Worship
00701801 . . . . $16.9●

Motown
00699734 . . . . $16.9●

The 1950s
00699922 . . . . $14.9●

The 1980s
00700551 . . . . $16.9●

Nirvana
00699762 . . . . $16.9●

Roy Orbison
00699752 . . . . $12.9●

Peter, Paul & Mary
00103013 . . . . $12.9●

Tom Petty
00699883 . . . . $15.9●

Pop/Rock
00699538 . . . . $14.9●

Praise & Worship
00699634 . . . . $14.9●

Elvis Presley
00699633 . . . . $14.9●

Queen
00702395 . . . . $12.9●

Red Hot Chili Peppers
00699710 . . . . $16.9●

Rock Ballads
00701034 . . . . $14.9●

Rock 'n' Roll
00699535 . . . . $14.9●

Bob Seger
00701147 . . . . $12.9●

Sting
00699921 . . . . $14.9●

Taylor Swift
00701799 . . . . $15.9●

Three Chord Songs
00699720 . . . . $12.9●

Top 100 Hymns Guitar Songbook
75718017 . . . . $12.9●

Ultimate-Guitar
00702617 . . . . $24.9●

Wedding Songs
00701005 . . . . $14.9●

Hank Williams
00700607 . . . . $14.9●

Neil Young–Decade
00700464 . . . . $14.9●

HAL•LEONARD®
CORPORATION

7777 W. BLUEMOUND RD. P.O. BOX 13819 MILWAUKEE, WI 53213

Visit Hal Leonard online at **www.halleonard.com**

081●